Healed from the Inside Out
Piece by Piece

by Naté

Inside Job
Healed from the Inside Out Piece by Piece
All Rights Reserved.
Copyright © 2024 Nate'
v1.0

The opinions expressed in this manuscript are solely the opinions of the author and do not represent the opinions or thoughts of the publisher. The author has represented and warranted full ownership and/or legal right to publish all the materials in this book.

This book may not be reproduced, transmitted, or stored in whole or in part by any means, including graphic, electronic, or mechanical without the express written consent of the publisher except in the case of brief quotations embodied in critical articles and reviews.

True Life Publishing

ISBN: 979-8-218-97670-5

Cover Photo © 2024 Nate'. All rights reserved - used with permission.

PRINTED IN THE UNITED STATES OF AMERICA

Table of Contents

FOREWORD

Are you ready to take your life back? This book Inside Job Healed Inside Out Piece by Piece is a courageous, transparent, transformative, and timely resource to do just that. Nate' courageously opens up about the trauma, abuse, and heartache she has experienced, taking us on a journey that, unfortunately, many of us may be able to relate to. This is not just another sad story. This is a book of hope, and it is written to equip you with the tools you need to take your life back, showing you that there is life after trauma and abuse.

Through the power of the Word of God, Nate' methodically guides you through the steps to transformation and true freedom. She shows you how to forgive and love yourself and others, drawing from her experiences of applying the Word of God, prayer, and counseling. She went from being a victim to becoming Victorious.

Many people suffer in silence for years due to trauma and abuse. It's time to find your voice and be free. This book may elicit tears, empathy, and even anger, but if you stick with it until the end, you will be empowered to be transformed.

Nate' is a beautiful and intelligent woman with a heart to see people set free from past trauma and abuse. I am humbled by Nate's courage, boldness, and tenacity. She is one of the most resilient women I have ever had the pleasure of knowing. Get ready to be transformed!

Pastor Kaylette Blunt

ACKNOWLEDGMENT

First and foremost, I express my heartfelt gratitude to my Lord and Savior. This project would not have been possible without you.

I want to express my immense gratitude towards my husband, Eugene. Throughout the process of completing this book, he has provided me with constant support and motivation. His unwavering faith in my abilities has been the driving force behind my dedication and perseverance. He has been a constant source of encouragement, standing by me every step of the way and cheering me on. His patience, sacrifices, understanding, and unconditional love have given me the necessary space and time to focus on this endeavor. I cannot thank him enough for his belief in me. My beloved husband, I am truly grateful for you being there for me.

I am grateful to Apostle Peter Taffe for being a source of inspiration and influencing the theological framework of my spiritual journey. Your valuable insights and perspectives have guided my thinking and contributed to the overall development of my spiritual growth. With love always, thank you!

I deeply appreciate Pastor Kaylette Blunt's support, review, feedback, and encouragement in the release of this book. Thank you, I love you!

I would like to express my heartfelt gratitude to Kandice Porter for her invaluable assistance in editing and proofreading this manuscript. Her keen attention to detail and unwavering commitment to improving the clarity and readability of the content have significantly enhanced the quality of this work. Thank you so much, Kandice. Your help is greatly appreciated, and I am deeply grateful for your dedication and hard work. I love you.

I would like to express my gratitude to my children for their continuous support, understanding, and patience throughout the process of writing this book. Your unwavering presence and support have provided me with the emotional stability and reassurance that I needed to navigate through this journey. Thank you for believing in me. I deeply love you.

Lastly, I would like to express my gratitude for the support and understanding of my family and friends. Their unwavering belief in my abilities has sustained me throughout this journey. Their encouragement, understanding, listening ear, provision of emotional support, and patience have given me the strength and confidence to overcome obstacles and pursue this journey with dedication.

INTRODUCTION

In this book, I want to share the calling that God has placed on my life and the purpose and direction that He has given me. I need to convey this so that readers can understand the journey I have been on and how it has shaped me.

One of the central themes in my life is the surrender of my will to God. I have willingly offered myself to be used for His Kingdom and believe that all kingdom business should be managed according to His ways and for His purposes. However, with this surrender comes the reality of increased exposure to the world and the enemy's attacks. Despite this, I have reached a point where I no longer feel ashamed of my past actions and behaviors. I have come to accept that they are a part of my journey, and I am fearless in the face of judgment.

Some may question why I have chosen to write about my life, especially considering that it hasn't always painted a positive picture of myself. Many may view my life through a distorted lens and judge me harshly. However, the answer is simple: it is not about my will, but about God's will. He sends us through trials and equips us with gifts to fulfill His purpose, not ours. Just as Jesus prayed in Luke 22:42, "Father, if you are willing, take this cup from me; yet not my will, but yours be done."

I am certain that the greater purpose of sharing my life story is to provide freedom and healing to others. The trauma I endured as a child, the ongoing abuse throughout my life, and the way I reacted to those experiences will be discussed in the upcoming chapters. While these events were meant to cause harm, God has turned them around for my good. Today, I have my own coaching business, a podcast focused on healing, and I serve as a speaker and advocate for abused and rape victims. Through my journey, I can walk alongside others in their healing process. I have become who I am today because of the storms I have weathered and the strength I have found to overcome. My struggles have not been in vain.

As described in 1 Corinthians 1:27, God often chooses the lowly and despised things of this world to nullify the things that are considered important. He finds treasures in unexpected places, even amid what may seem like trash. He didn't take the obvious route to find a treasure that He could use. Instead, He came to me in my mess and rescued me from the clutches of the enemy.

I have lived through verbal, mental, and physical abuse from a young age, which led me to believe that dysfunction was a normal way of life. I always hoped things would turn out differently, but they never did. I searched for happiness in different things and people, depending on them to make me feel fulfilled, rather than finding happiness within myself. This led me into unhealthy relationships that often involved some form of abuse. I loved deeply and expected the same in return, but I was coming from a place of brokenness and didn't truly understand what love looked like.

I was abusing prescription medication, using it to numb myself and escape from reality. I reached the end of myself and attempted suicide. Although I was not successful, I became very sick and had to be treated in the hospital. It felt like darkness surrounded me. I was emotionally drained, constantly crying, and experiencing hallucinations. I was unable to function in my day-to-day life and felt hopeless.

But in that dark moment, I started to see glimpses of light and began to feel better about myself. I realized that the only answer I had was God. The pills were no longer working, people had distanced themselves from me, and I had hit rock bottom. Today, I can proudly say that I am completely healed in the areas where I once struggled. I am free from the feelings of rejection, hopelessness, and brokenness. My relationship with God is amazing, and I am living my life with purpose and passion. Through my story, those who don't know me will come to understand the power of God in my life, and those who do know me will gain a deeper understanding of why I am the way I am.

God desires for us to love others unconditionally and with compassion. When we do this, we reflect the love and grace of our God to those who are lost and broken. While I hope that reading my story will inspire and celebrate my deliverance, my ultimate desire is for readers to have a personal experience with God. It is through personal experiences that our beliefs are truly impacted and transformed.

One of the most powerful truths that I hold onto is found in Jeremiah 29:11, where God declares that He knows the thoughts He thinks towards us—thoughts of peace, not of evil, and plans to give us a future and hope. This verse reminds me that God has a purpose and a plan for each of our lives, and it is filled with goodness and hope.

Nonetheless, Satan, in his attempts to discredit the call of God on my life, would often remind me of my struggle with memorization. Satan would constantly whisper in my ear, telling me that I was nothing and a failure. He would manipulate and distort the words that God had spoken to me about myself. The most dangerous weapon he used was my mind. When he could infiltrate my thoughts and change my thinking patterns, I would miss the mark on everything God had already declared about me. For a while, I was trapped in a place of distraction and confusion.

During the traumatic times in my childhood, I was vulnerable to the influence of evil spirits. These demonic forces planted seeds of rejection within me, causing me to feel ashamed, hateful, and bitter. It is important to remember that our battle is not against flesh and blood, but against spiritual forces of darkness. As Ephesians 6:12 states, we wrestle against principalities, powers, and spiritual wickedness in high places. These forces seek to distort our identity and keep us from fulfilling our purpose in God.

However, my purpose is to serve the Lord, and I firmly believe that what His word has declared about me will become a reality in my life. I am determined to align my thoughts and beliefs with the truth of God's word, rejecting the lies and manipulations of the enemy. I trust that God's plans for me are good, and I am committed to walking in His purpose and fulfilling His calling on my life.

1
THE YOUNGER DAYS

From the moment I was conceived, my life seemed to be marked by pain and trauma. As the youngest of three daughters, I was not the son my parents had hoped for. My mother shared with me the disappointment my dad had when he found out I was another girl. He didn't accept it so much to the point, he bought boy attire for me even knowing I was a girl. While I believed my parents loved me, there was always a sense of disappointment that I carried with me.

Growing up, I often felt like an only child because my sisters were much older than me. I spent a lot of time playing by myself, which could be lonely at times. But it was at the age of five that my life took a dark turn. I was molested, and this abuse continued for several years. The abuse started with just sitting on my dad's friend's lap between his legs but soon escalated to more aggressive and graphic acts. My dad's friend would manipulate me with promises of candy and threats of getting into trouble if I told anyone. I was only five years old, and the fear consumed me.

I resented my dad for constantly exposing me to these dangerous situations. Deep down, I suspected that he was aware of what was happening. My sisters always thought I was daddy's girl but what they did not know was the abuse that was happening every time I was with my dad.

Around the same time, I was also subjected to abuse by a female friend of my father's. She had a daughter who was close to my age, and she would touch me inappropriately. Eventually, she encouraged me and her daughter to engage in inappropriate acts while she watched. I cried every time and didn't want it but the fear of punishment and the beatings her children endured kept me silent. This became a twisted normalcy in my life. Whenever I went to their house, I knew that something inappropriate would happen. It continued for years, even when the daughter would come to my house. I remember my sisters caught us once, unclothed and messing around with one another. I was filled with shame and fear of being exposed. They would call me names and tease me for being "nasty". They didn't know that I had been subjected to this abuse for years and was just doing what was normal to me. I was too young at the time to explain that to them, plus I didn't want to tell them because I was afraid, I'd get in trouble.

By the age of eleven, I despised my life and myself. The depression began to take hold, and I began to draw into seclusion. My mother, who worked tirelessly to provide for us, didn't realize the extent of my pain. She trusted my father to take care of me, unaware of the horrors I was enduring. I don't blame her for any of it. She did the best she could with the circumstances she faced. She knew something was wrong with her baby girl who cried often and became afraid of anything that moved. That was the first time of many that I started seeing a therapist. Even inside of therapy, at that age, I wasn't convinced that I'd be safe if I talked about the abuse, so therapy wasn't working for me then.

At thirteen, I experienced the worst abuse of all. I was babysitting for one of my dad's friends. Late one night, he returned home drunk and entered the room where I was sleeping in the same bed as his children. He covered my mouth with his hand, threatened me with a knife, and pulled me out of the bed onto the floor. He raped me, leaving me traumatized and terrified. He warned me not to tell anyone, threatening to harm me and my mother if I did. That same abuse at knifepoint became a pattern for him over many years until one day I said to my mother, I do not want to babysit anymore. I blamed it on the kids being bad and too much for me to manage and I didn't have to go back. I recall him re-enforcing his threat that even though I was not watching the kids any longer if I told on him, he would harm my mother and I believed him. So, I did not tell. I carried that secret with me for years, living in constant fear and shame.

Amidst the abuse, at age fifteen I started liking boys willingly. Still timid and afraid of speaking up I would have unprotected sex and became pregnant by my boyfriend. I was a freshman in high school. I continued with my education at an alternative school for pregnant girls. For a moment, I had a reprieve from the abuse because of the pregnancy. I was having a son. Excited and scared at the same time, I was just a child myself. I had him at the age of sixteen.

I thought things were on the rise for me. I had a handsome son; he had just turned a year old. I was in school, working, and just pressing forward. Destruction would make its way to me soon thereafter. The abuse started up again but this time closer to home. We had always been a close-knit family so being with and hanging out with our cousins was something we all did regularly on both sides of the family. I would soon become a victim of incest. One of my male cousins began to touch me inappropriately and make unwanted comments. It ultimately ended with him having sex with me. Despite being older, I felt powerless to stop it. Though he did not threaten me, I still had an enormous amount of fear of what would happen if I told on him. It only happened once as he saw how uncomfortable I was around him and I cannot help but think maybe someone else could see that and make a connection that something had happened. The shame and self-blame consumed me, leading me further into depression because here again, I found myself being abused and not telling anyone. Just going along with it. I started questioning myself and blaming myself that I must be doing something for this to continue to happen to me. I felt as though I wore a neon sign that said, "I'm easy and won't tell." What was drawing men to abuse me? I know for certain that I was not the initiator. I was not having sexual conversations, wearing provocative attire, or asking for them to have sex with me. So why me, I asked. That question led me to withdraw from being around people and it began impacting my mental and emotional self.

I attempted suicide multiple times, believing that this cycle of abuse would never end. The self-criticism and self-hatred were over-whelming. I blamed myself for allowing the abuse to happen, even though I was just a child. I blamed myself for not telling anyone. The fear and trauma paralyzed me, preventing me from seeking help or speaking out for years.

It was not until my early 20s that I found myself reflecting on the numerous instances of sexual assault and unwanted sexual en-counters I had experienced. Determined to take control of my life, I decided to stand up for myself and put an end to the abuse I was do-ing to myself. I found the courage to finally share what happened to me. Looking back, I realized that the abuse had stolen my voice and my sense of self-worth. I had to confront the deep-rooted shame and guilt that had plagued me for so long. I eventually sought ther-apy and support from loved ones which played a crucial role in my healing journey.

I had to learn to separate my worth from the abuse I endured. I began to see that I was no longer going to be defined by the pain of my past. It had been a long and difficult journey, but I was deter-mined to reclaim my life and find joy and peace.

If you are a survivor of abuse, know that you are not alone. Healing is possible, and there is support available to you. Reach out to trusted friends, family, or professionals who can help you navigate your healing journey. You are deserving of love, happiness, and a life free from the pain of your past.

2
I'M OLDER NOW

I spent the first half of my twenties focusing on healing. Collaborating with multiple counselors and reading self-help books. I was feeling better than I had felt in a long time. I met and fell in "love" with a man. He showed me a love that didn't come with force. The relationship thrived for several years. Just as I thought the abuse had stopped, it didn't. It just transformed into a different form. I found myself having mental breakdowns. It was more than I was willing to endure so I decided to leave him. It wasn't an easy transition.

After moving on from this relationship, it sent me back into a battle of depression. I started back therapy and felt I had a bigger hill to climb because now I'm a single mother of two. Trying to balance work and being a mother. I was angry all the time. I was exhausted in the attempt to fix a life that I did not break. It was so unfair to me that I had to fight so hard to be happy and at peace. I was a broken woman. Counseling wasn't moving fast enough for me, so I started trying to self-medicate again. I started drinking a lot this time. It did nothing but make things worse.

A few years later, I decided to start going to church. Looking for help in a different way than I had tried. I knew something had to change, perhaps me! It moved the needle a bit for me, and things started to look bright again. It wasn't long before I had another love interest. We dated for a while, spending a lot of time with one another, enjoying life and having fun. When we met, he was in the middle of a divorce. Hindsight, that was my first mistake. A broken woman gave a broken man the time of day, but we kept it going. I believed him when he said it was over with him and his ex, however, I would later find out that wasn't all true. However, he did end up getting a divorce.

We continued to date, and he would eventually move in with me. Out of one house from his family straight into my home with my kids. Mistake number two for me. We loved each other and we introduced our kids to one another, and they would get along and it all worked. There were problems in between with this ex at times but nothing we couldn't work through. A year later we married, and we added to our family. Life was going well. We bought our first home together. You couldn't tell me that he wasn't the man I'd spend the rest of my life with. We were deeply in love and created a blended family that looked like ease. We were young, but our love for each other and our children was all-consuming. Married life felt beautiful, and I loved my husband with every fiber of my being.

Like any relationship, we faced our fair share of ups and downs, but our strong bond and love for each other helped us weather those small storms. However, as time went on, external influences began to chip away at our relationship. What I thought was a fairytale love, was more of a disaster than I knew. My husband had been having an affair with many other women from the early days of our marriage. Unfortunately, his betrayal and deception ultimately led me to file for divorce.

Seems contradictory when I say we had a deep love for one another, maybe even delusional right? To shed some light on that, I did not know of any of the affairs until about the 9th year of marriage. He showed me a lot of love despite his infidelity. One may think, certainly there were some red flags that I just ignored. Nope! Not that I saw. I'm not the nagging type and I trusted him so when he said he was with his friends, I believed him. When he said he was at work, I believed him. So, blinded by brokenness? Maybe!

The pain of the divorce was almost unbearable for me. It felt like I was suffocating. The timing of the divorce was particularly difficult, as it occurred shortly within months of the passing of my mother and amid my father's declining health. Losing my mother had already brought me to a low point in my life, but the divorce pushed me even further down.

Grieving the loss of my mother, dealing with the aftermath of the divorce, and preparing for my father's death took a tremendous toll on my mental health. I thought I had a handle on my depression, but it became clear that it still had a hold on me. I was devastated! A divorce and two deaths in the same year! Yeah, I was devastated!

My mother's death was the snowball effect that triggered downhill for me. It was October 2009. She was diagnosed with gastric cancer. She underwent chemotherapy and had surgery to remove 85% of her stomach. It was successful. We celebrated her life and gave her flowers. We thought we were on the road to recovery, but in 2011, cancer returned, and the doctors told us there was nothing more they could do. My mother was at stage 4, and the cancer was aggressive. It was a devastating blow, and I struggled to come to terms with the reality of the situation.

Despite the dire prognosis, my mother displayed incredible strength and acceptance. She chose to live the rest of her life in peace and made the most of the time she had left. I remember sitting with her and my sisters, planning her funeral. It was a bittersweet moment as we tried to honor her wishes while grappling with the pain of losing her. I tried to be strong for her, hiding my tears and breaking down in private.

As the days passed, my mother's health deteriorated rapidly. She needed constant care. My sisters, my aunt, and I took shifts to ensure she was comfortable. It was a challenging and emotionally draining experience. I found myself slipping into a deep depression, struggling to sleep and losing interest in the things I once enjoyed. Watching my mother lose her memory and become completely dependent on us for care was heartbreaking.

Again, depression consumed me, and I felt lost without my mother. She had always been my rock, my confidant, and my best friend. The thought of facing life without her was terrifying. I was angry and heartbroken, and I didn't know how to cope with the pain. On top of that, there was a secret that my mother and I had kept hidden for years.

During this difficult time, I began to hear the voice of God. I pleaded with Him to keep my mother alive, but He reminded me that He was my provider, confidant, and friend. He urged me to put my trust in Him. To distract myself from watching my mother's decline, I started making encouraging greeting cards and writing messages that I needed to hear myself. It kept me busy, but the depression still weighed heavily on me.

The day before my mother passed away, I fasted and prayed for a miracle. I held onto hope, believing that God could perform wonders. But deep down, I hadn't fully accepted the reality of the situation. When I showed my mother the greeting cards, I could see the pride in her eyes, even though she couldn't speak. It was a powerful moment, but it was also heartbreaking. I ran out of the room, trying to be strong, but moments later, she passed away. I was devastated!

The secret that my mother and I had kept for so long was my struggle with depression. It started when I was just eleven years old, I was seeing a therapist. She kept it hidden, afraid of judgment and rejection. I learned to hide my depression, fearing how others would view me. It wasn't until later, when I sought help from a psychiatrist, that I discovered I had major depression. I had suffered in silence for years, and the extent of my struggle was known to only me and my mom.

Without proper treatment, my disorder worsened, and I again turned to prescription drugs and alcohol to numb the pain. I hid it well, I just wanted all the pain to go away, but it only spiraled me further into darkness. I took risks with recreational drugs as well, desperate to escape the turmoil within my soul. It felt like I had lost total control.

I was in bad shape. I reached out for help. Seeing my therapist weekly, he suggested I take a leave of absence to regain control. I did just that! I honestly didn't care at the time if I lost my job or not. Even though I had my children and grandchildren, I still felt hopeless.

Within a year in and out of the hospital from mental/nervous breakdowns, I was finally able to pull it together. I went back to work and began attending church regularly. I joined the praise and worship team and even did some interpretive dancing. I became fully engaged in the word. It was ultimately what saved my life from the burning hell I was in. During my journey, my relationship with God and my relationship with myself grew tremendously. I not only fell in love with myself, but I fell in love with God. It was in this time frame that I heard God call me to write my book. It was during this time that I began hearing more and more of God's voice and instruction. I wrote several songs inside this desolate place. In writing this book, God sent me through several steps that you will read the chapters to follow.

3
THE HEALING PROCESS

The beginning of my healing journey may differ from yours, but I firmly believe that God is not partial to certain individuals. What He has done for me, He can do for you in a way that is uniquely designed for your personal growth and transformation.

To experience God's healing power, I had to first confront and take responsibility for my past actions and the person I used to be. I had to shift my mindset from a self-centred perspective of what's in it for me, to a mindset of trust and surrender, believing that God has a plan for my life. I sought to develop a deeper relationship with God, seeking to understand His true nature and character. This involved reading the Bible and immersing myself in His teachings, allowing His words to guide and shape my thoughts and actions.

Prayer became an essential part of my daily routine, although initially, I struggled with the idea of what a "proper" prayer should look like. I soon realized that prayer is not about using fancy words or following a specific formula, but rather about opening my heart and expressing my genuine needs and desires to God. Even a simple plea of "Help me, Lord!" is enough for God to hear and understand the depths of my struggles.

Through this process of seeking a deeper relationship with God, I discovered that His love and grace are boundless. He met me in my brokenness and provided the healing and restoration that I desperately needed. It was not an overnight transformation, but a gradual journey of surrendering my will to His and allowing Him to work in and through me.

I encourage you to embark on your journey of seeking a deeper relationship with God. Open your heart to His love and guidance, and trust that He has a unique plan for your healing and growth. Remember, God is not limited by our circumstances or past mistakes. He is ready and willing to meet you where you are and lead you toward a life of wholeness and purpose.

As you read through the next seven components of the healing process (rejection, forgiveness, gentleness, patience, obedience, trust, and love) that God took me through, I pray they will enlighten you. Take your time and read the scriptures and prayers.

COMPONENT 1
REJECTION

Psalm 34:17-20
The righteous cry out, and the LORD hears them;
he delivers them from all their troubles. The LORD is close
to the broken-hearted and saves those who are crushed
in spirit. The righteous person may have many troubles,
but the LORD delivers him from them all; he protects
all his bones, not one of them will be broken.

Rejection is a deeply painful experience that can have a significant impact on our emotional well-being. From a young age, I felt the sting of rejection, and it became crucial for me to understand its effects and how to heal from it. I embarked on a journey of self-discovery, seeking to unravel the complexities of rejection and why it hurt so deeply.

Through my research, I discovered that our brains are wired to respond to rejection in a similar way to physical pain. Studies have shown that the same area of our brain that processes physical pain becomes activated when we experience rejection. This explains why even small rejections can feel so overwhelmingly painful, as they elicit a genuine emotional response.

The impact of rejection extends beyond emotional pain. It can damage our mood, lower our self-esteem, and trigger feelings of anger and aggression. Rejection also disrupts our innate need for belonging, leaving us vulnerable and questioning our worthiness of love and acceptance.

One of the most damaging aspects of rejection is often self-inflicted. In the aftermath of rejection, it is common to engage in self-criticism and negative self-talk. I found myself calling myself names, dwelling on my shortcomings, and feeling disgusted with myself. This pattern of self-destructive behavior only exacerbated the emotional pain I was already experiencing.

To break free from this cycle, I realized the importance of creating a plan to help me move forward. I took the time to reflect and wrote down in my journal what I would do differently each day of the week. This plan served as a roadmap for my healing journey and helped me reprogram my mind to think positively when negative thoughts arose.

I also recognized that changing my mindset was not enough. I needed to create an environment that supported my growth and healing. Just as a recovering alcoholic would struggle to overcome their addiction in a room full of liquor, I needed to surround myself with positivity and remove myself from toxic influences.

After going through a divorce, rejection had a profound impact on my self-esteem. I felt abandoned, alone, and hopeless. I blamed myself for the failed relationship and struggled to find balance in my life. It seemed impossible to bring myself back into alignment and I questioned God's role in my life. I was angry at Him for not answering my prayers to reconcile with my husband and felt that He had abandoned me as well.

In this state of rejection, I found myself engaging in unhealthy behaviors. I turned to drinking again and even had thoughts of suicide. I knew I couldn't stay in that dark place, or I would end up dead. It was at this point that I surrendered and allowed God to help me.

Rejection can have a profound impact on our lives, but it is possible to heal and move forward. It requires self-reflection, seeking professional help, and surrounding ourselves with supportive and understanding individuals. By prioritizing our well-being and taking the necessary steps toward healing, we can overcome the effects of rejection and find hope and happiness once again.

Surrounding myself with a supportive and understanding community was also crucial in my healing journey. I sought out friends and loved ones who could empathize with my experiences and provide a listening ear and a shoulder to lean on. Their love, encouragement, and support played a significant role in my healing process.

I also turned to my faith for strength and guidance. I found solace in prayer, meditation, and reading scripture. I leaned on God's promises of healing and restoration, and I trusted that He would walk with me every step of the way.

Healing from rejection is not a linear process. There were setbacks and moments of doubt along the way. But I remained committed to my healing journey and reminded myself of how far I had come. I celebrated every small victory and used setbacks as opportunities for growth and learning.

Today, I can confidently say that I have healed from the effects of rejection. While the scars may still be there, they no longer define me. I have learned to embrace my worthiness of love and acceptance, and I have found peace within myself.

If you are struggling with the effects of rejection, know that healing is possible. It may be a challenging and painful journey, but with the right support, self-reflection, and a commitment to forgiveness, you can overcome the pain and find healing and restoration. You are worthy of love and acceptance, and you have the strength within you to heal and thrive.

Prayer

Heavenly Father, I thank you for showing me who you have called me to be. I pray against the rejection that keeps me in bondage and clouds my ability to receive your truth. I ask that you use this day to remind me of your love and your words over me.

I pray for discernment to recognize the enemy's lies. Give me eyes to see myself how you see me. I thank you,

God, that rejection is not from you. I praise you for loving me despite my flaws and shortcomings. Thank you for seeing my heart and molding my life to reflect you. With breathless wonder, I give you all my faith, all my hope, and all my love. I ask this of your matchless name. Amen

COMPONENT 2
FORGIVENESS

Colossians 3:13
"Bear with each other and forgive one another
if any of you has a grievance against someone.
Forgive as the Lord forgave you."

The journey of forgiveness has had a significant impact on my life. I struggled with forgiving myself because I believed that I should have been stronger and more vocal about the abuse I experienced, especially as I grew older. These feelings weighed heavily on me for years, leading to anger, outrageous behavior, and a sense of injustice. I even found myself angry at God for allowing this trauma to happen to me when I was just a helpless child.

Forgiving those who wronged me was also challenging because I didn't feel they deserved it. Holding onto unforgiveness only fueled my anger, fear, sadness, resentment, and desire for revenge. This negativity took a toll on my mental and physical health, resulting in depression, digestive issues, hair loss, and frequent illness.

However, I have come to realize that forgiveness starts within us. When God revealed to me the depth of my wrongdoing, it was a painful and humbling experience. I spent weeks crying, overwhelmed by the sadness of the life I had lived and the pain I had caused others. But through this revelation, I also discovered the love and forgiveness I needed to extend to myself. I had to let go of the blame I placed on myself for not speaking up about the abuse. Therapy helped me understand that none of it was my fault, and I couldn't change what had happened.

This realization brought a sense of relief and lifted the burden of self-hate and negative emotions. I learned to accept that the abuse happened, but I didn't have to agree with it or let it define me. In my journey of self-forgiveness, I have come to understand that it was God who initiated this process within me. I believe that there is still work to be done in forgiving myself, particularly concerning the emotions I have carried from my childhood. Initially, I had to gain an understanding that the experiences I went through as a child were not my fault. This understanding was facilitated through therapy and reading the Bible. At first, I resented myself for seemingly accepting what had happened without taking any action. I remember feeling overwhelmed and questioning why God couldn't just take away the pain and allow me to love myself. However, I soon realized that this journey towards self-forgiveness would be a long and challenging one.

As an adult, the process of understanding and forgiving myself has been even more difficult. I have made choices that have led me to feel anger towards myself, such as entering unhealthy relationships or staying in situations when it was time to leave. There are moments when I still find myself experiencing regret, reminding me that I need to continue working on forgiving myself every day. It can be an arduous task, but I am committed to it.

Understanding forgiveness has been a crucial part of my healing journey. I have learned that forgiving others does not mean condoning their actions or trusting them again. It is about releasing the anger and hurt they have caused me and finding freedom from the pain. I have had to forgive the same person multiple times until talking about what they have done no longer brings me pain. This process was particularly challenging during my divorce, but with time and therapy, I was able to forgive and move forward.

It is important to note that forgiveness does not mean forgetting or denying reality. It is not the same as reconciling or excusing someone's actions. Forgiveness is a personal decision that starts with a change in attitude. It is not always necessary to communicate our forgiveness to the person who hurt us. Holding onto unforgiveness only keeps us trapped in a cycle of pain and resentment. Once I understood these concepts, it became easier to forgive and follow the example set by the Lord's Prayer, asking God to forgive us as we forgive others.

I would also pray this prayer over myself:

> *Dear Heavenly Father, I understand that there is nothing to gain by holding myself in unforgiveness and there is everything to gain by releasing myself from unforgiveness and beginning the process of healing. I want to move forward and make a positive difference in the future. I confess the ungodly accountability, self-abasement, and the vows I have made to never forgive myself. Because Jesus died for my sins, I choose to forgive myself—to no longer punish myself and be angry with myself. I forgive myself for letting this hurt control me and for hurting others out of my hurt. I repent of this behavior and my attitude. I ask for Your forgiveness and healing. God, help me to NEVER again retain unforgiveness of myself or others. Thank you for loving me and for Your grace to move forward with You. In Jesus' Name, Amen.*

I want to emphasize that forgiveness is not a simple or easy process. It requires time, self-reflection, and a willingness to let go of perceived power. But through my journey, I have experienced the transformative power of forgiveness and the freedom it brings.

To be completely honest, it took me about a year, if not a little longer, to truly be able to walk in forgiveness after my divorce. It was a similar timeframe with my abusers, but that was because initially, I didn't know how to forgive or even want to. However, once I made the decision to forgive them, it took about a year or so before I began to see results.

There were many times when I wanted to give up, but I didn't, and God wouldn't allow me to. He kept placing me in situations where I needed to forgive others or make mature decisions that required instant forgiveness. I had to break free from the victim mentality and face those I was upset with, even though I didn't like it. I knew I was called to be loving, kind, and forgiving, even when I didn't believe they deserved it. It was frustrating, especially when I had to see my ex-husband with another woman at our children's parties or events while I was still heartbroken and alone. But I had to walk in that situation with grace. I would only speak if spoken to, and it took time for me to mature enough to initiate conversation. It wasn't easy, and it certainly didn't happen overnight. However, I eventually reached a point where I truly understood forgiveness and could forgive from a pure heart.

Pure-hearted forgiveness goes beyond simply saying, "I'm done with it," and avoiding the person. It allows you to be in any space they are in, no matter what, with a genuine smile and without being spiteful or mean. You can even initiate conversation or offer a kind gesture. You can be in their presence as if nothing ever happened. This doesn't mean that what they did is erased or that you condone their actions. It simply means that the pain no longer resides within you. It's a choice you make to let go and not carry the burden of unforgiveness. However, it's important to note that both parties need to be ready for forgiveness. Until you're ready, you may struggle and easily fall back into an unforgiving state. Forgiveness is a process.

I found that forgiveness not only made way for happiness but also for health and peace. It led to healthier relationships, psychological well-being, lower blood pressure, and higher self-esteem. It even helped alleviate my depression, which had been very unhealthy for me. Holding onto unforgiveness can weaken your immune system and increase anxiety and stress levels. In my 30s, I realized the reality of these effects, and it became essential for me to forgive. I went through a significant period of growth during that time.

Letting go and forgiving no longer defined my life by how I had been hurt. I was able to find compassion and understanding for those who had hurt me. I realized that we never truly know what someone else is dealing with or what they have been through. This doesn't justify their actions but being enlightened by this truth made it easier for me to deal with.

As Dr. Martin Luther King Jr. once said, "We must develop and maintain the capacity to forgive. He who is devoid of the power to forgive is devoid of the power to love."

Forgiveness is not always easy, and it is a process that takes time and effort. However, the rewards of forgiveness are immeasurable. It brings healing, happiness, and a deeper connection with God and others. I encourage you to embark on your journey of forgiveness and experience the transformative power it holds.

Prayer

Heavenly Father, you are a forgiving and merciful God, abounding in love to all who call upon you. Thank you for granting forgiveness so freely to us who are so undeserving. I pray that you'll overwhelm us with awareness of how much we've been forgiven and that we'll be able to grant the same mercy to others who have wronged us. Open our eyes to the trap caused by bitterness and enable us to find freedom by following your example. In your matchless name, I pray. Amen.

COMPONENT 3
GENTLENESS

Galatians 6:1
Brothers, if anyone is caught in any transgression,
you who are spiritual should restore him in a spirit
of gentleness. Keep watch on yourself,
lest you too be tempted.

Gentleness is often referred to as meekness, but it should not be mistaken for weakness. It encompasses humility, gratitude towards God, and respectful behavior towards others. The opposite of gentleness includes anger, a desire for revenge, and self-centeredness. Gentleness is a display of strength under control. It allows us to be tender and compassionate, mirroring the immense power and vastness of God.

Understanding gentleness requires trusting that God will ensure justice, and it necessitates a correct perception of who God is and our identity in Him. It takes a truly strong individual to embody gentleness. It is a lesson that I had to learn through personal experiences and self-reflection.

As I began to extend gentleness towards myself, I realized the importance of self-compassion. I had to let go of the self-blame and harsh criticism that I had internalized. I learned to treat myself with kindness and understanding, acknowledging that I am not defined by my past experiences or the opinions of others. This shift in mindset allowed me to heal and grow, and it also enabled me to extend gentleness towards others.

In the past, anger was my default emotion, and I would use it without hesitation. It didn't matter where I was, whether it was in traffic, at the supermarket, or at the doctor's office. If I felt disrespected or hurt, I would lash out. I vividly remember a particular incident at the supermarket where someone thought they got to a parking space before me, even though I had my blinker on. I turned into the space, and before I knew it, the woman came over and kicked my tire, hurling insults at me. In that moment, I wasn't in a healed space, and my immediate response was to retaliate in a similar manner. I unleashed my anger not only on her but also on everyone else who had wronged me. Looking back, I realize that my actions were wrong. I could have chosen a different approach, such as calling the police, but I didn't. Instead, I engaged in a physical altercation with her in the parking lot. If I had the chance to meet her today, I would apologize and explain that I have grown and changed since that incident. I would assure her that the person I am today would handle the situation differently.

Gentleness allows us to be tender and compassionate, just like how we perceive the immense power and vastness of God. God, who is greater than the universe and transcends space and time, treats us with utmost tenderness and care. Understanding gentleness requires trusting that God will ensure justice and having a correct perception of who God is and our identity in Him.

Embodying gentleness is not an easy task, especially in a world that often values strength and toughness. However, it is a lesson worth learning. It teaches us to approach ourselves and others with kindness, compassion, and understanding. It reminds us to set boundaries and stand up for ourselves and others, but to do so with grace and empathy. Gentleness has the power to bring healing, love, and peace into our lives and the lives of those around us. It is a lesson that continues to shape and guide me, reminding me to have a strong hand and a soft touch in all my interactions.

As I reflect on my past reckless behavior and the times when I failed to seek God's guidance in moments of hurt, I am amazed by His protection and grace. It is truly a miracle that I am not in a jail cell or worse, in a grave. His tenderness and care extend far beyond my comprehension. I didn't even believe that I deserved to be saved. There were countless fights and situations where I lost control, but God still saved me.

Despite my angry state, God didn't treat me the way I treated others. His unconditional love has transformed me into the person I am today. I have learned to turn challenging situations into teaching moments, sharing the healing power of God's love with those who are hurting and lashing out. I have come to understand that gentleness is not a sign of weakness, but rather a strength that comes from trusting in God's justice.

I often rely on this lesson of gentleness with my children, as they have a way of pushing our emotional intelligence to its limits. Even in moments of frustration, I choose gentleness over anger, knowing that it reflects my identity as a child of God. Embodying gentleness requires strength and the correct understanding of who God is and who we are in Him.

Truly embracing gentleness is a continuous journey, but it brings healing and peace into our lives and the lives of those around us. It is a testament to the power of God's love and the transformation it can bring.

Gentleness is one of the fruits of the Spirit, and I have chosen to back it with a bunch of scripture. However, practicing gentleness is not always easy, especially when we have experienced deep pain and betrayal. The pain of betrayal can feel like our hearts being ground to crumbs, making it difficult to show kindness to those who have hurt us.

I can relate to this feeling of betrayal and the desire for revenge. I have personally experienced the pain of being betrayed by my ex-husband, and it felt like my heart was being run through a meat grinder. It is natural to question why we should be kind to someone who has violated us or threatened our lives or the lives of our loved ones. How can we show gentleness to someone who has molested and raped us repeatedly, while also threatening our family if we were to speak out? How can we show gentleness toward someone who has betrayed us?

I remember a specific instance when my ex-husband showed up at my mother's funeral. The anger and pain I felt at that moment made me want to inflict the same amount of pain on him that he had caused me. I wanted to make him understand the depth of the hurt he had caused. However, as a follower of God, I knew that I should strive to show kindness and forgiveness, even in the face of such betrayal.

I tried my best to be kind on many occasions, but I also failed many times. At the funeral, I couldn't bring myself to embrace him or even acknowledge his presence. I gave him the coldest cold shoulder and stared him down because I believed he didn't deserve any kindness or forgiveness. While I don't think I should have forced myself to accept his embrace, I missed an opportunity to show forgiveness and release some of the internal rage I was carrying.

It wasn't until I experienced freedom from the bondage of rejection and truly forgave my offender that I felt led to be gentle and kind towards him. Surprisingly, it wasn't as difficult as I anticipated. I have always been a kind and gentle soul, so shedding that part of me was just a test to see if I had truly forgiven him. God filled me with gentleness, making it a natural response to extend kindness to those I had forgiven.

A few months after my mother's passing, my father also passed away. It was during his funeral that I saw my offender again. This time, he chose not to extend his hand to me, but I took the opportunity to tell him that I had forgiven him for his wrongdoing and that vengeance would be in God's hands. It felt incredibly liberating to express my forgiveness and let go of the hostility I had carried towards him.

I credit God for walking me through this journey of forgiveness and gentleness. It was through His word and the trials I faced that I was able to find the strength to show kindness even to those who had hurt me deeply. It is a testament to the transformative power of God's love and the fruit of the Spirit working in our lives.

The power of our words and actions is undeniable. We can influence others through what we say and how we behave. However, with this power comes great responsibility. Gentleness serves as a constraint and channel for this power. It is the recognition that God's ways and thoughts are higher than our own, as stated in Isaiah 55:9. It is a humble acknowledgment that our worldviews can be shaped by sin and the misinterpretation of our experiences. To be gentle is to accept God's worldview, reflecting the truth about the spiritual and material realms.

When we are filled with the fruit of gentleness, which is a result of the Holy Spirit's work in our lives, we approach correction with ease instead of engaging in arguments fueled by resentment and anger. We understand that the salvation of others is far more important than our pride, as mentioned in 2 Timothy 2:24-25. I have personally experienced the power of gentleness in my own life, particularly during my divorce. Instead of engaging in heated arguments over material possessions, I chose to have cordial conversations and express what I believed to be a fair resolution. By approaching the situation with gentleness, it disarmed my ex-spouse from being defensive, and ultimately, I was able to achieve a fair outcome. It was a lesson in setting aside my pride and focusing on what truly mattered.

Gentleness is a virtue that has the power to transform our lives and the lives of those around us. It reflects God's character and is a testament to His love and grace. When we embrace gentleness, we can forgive others, recognize the importance of unity, and humbly submit to God's will.

One of the key aspects of gentleness is the willingness to forgive others. In Matthew 18:23-35, Jesus tells the parable of the unforgiving servant to illustrate the importance of forgiveness. The servant in the parable owed a great debt to his master, but when he was unable to pay, the master forgave him. However, the servant then refused to forgive a fellow servant who owed him a much smaller debt. This parable reminds us that we have been forgiven by God for our sins, and therefore, we should extend that same forgiveness to others.

Gentleness also eradicates competition and sectarianism. In Philippians 1:15-18, Paul addresses the issue of rivalry among preachers. He emphasizes that the goal should be the advancement of the gospel, rather than personal gain or recognition. When we embrace gentleness, we shift our focus from ourselves to the proclamation of the gospel, allowing unity and collaboration to take precedence over competition.

John the Baptist serves as an example of gentleness, despite his fiery preaching style. In John 3:30, he humbly states, "[Jesus] must become greater; I must become less." This demonstrates his willingness to step aside and let Jesus take center stage. It is a reminder that gentleness involves putting aside our desires and ego and allowing God to be exalted.

In my own life, I have experienced the transformative power of gentleness. As I studied passages that emphasized the importance of gentleness, I realized that it was a virtue that God desired for me to cultivate. Through His power and guidance, I was able to let go of anger and bitterness and embrace gentleness. It was a profound shift that allowed me to love others and extend grace and compassion, even in the face of adversity.

Gentleness is not a sign of weakness, but rather an attribute of God's strength working within us. It takes strength to choose gentleness over cruelty, to respond with kindness instead of anger. It reflects the strength that comes from God, enabling us to love others in a way that we could not have done on our own.

In conclusion, gentleness is a powerful virtue that can transform our lives and the lives of those around us. It requires us to forgive others, embrace unity, and humbly submit to God's will. When we cultivate gentleness, we reflect the character of Christ and allow His love and grace to shine through us. May we strive to embrace gentleness in all areas of our lives, allowing it to guide our relationships and interactions with others.

Prayer

Heavenly Father,

We come before you with gratitude for all that you are, for all that you have given us, for your mercy and grace towards us, for your presence and faithfulness. You created us to reflect your image and in doing so, to bring you glory. We confess to you that we fail to do this. Every day, we fall short. In our words, our actions, and in our thoughts, we lift ourselves and create things instead of you. Thank you for your unfailing patience with us. Thank you for your gentleness with our stubborn and rebellious hearts.

Help us to be careful with our responses and interactions with others. Help us to be those who bring calm to the storms raging in this world. We ask this in your matchless name.

Amen!

COMPONENT 4
PATIENCE

Patience is a virtue that can be challenging to cultivate, especially in a world that values instant gratification. It requires us to accept delays, troubles, and suffering without becoming angry or upset. However, practicing patience is essential for our growth and well-being.

In my journey, I realized that impatience was a characteristic deeply ingrained within me. I had always been accustomed to getting what I wanted when I wanted it. This entitlement mentality stemmed from a place of feeling like a victim and seeking validation through material possessions and the approval of others. However, this mindset only fueled the cycle of rejection and hindered my personal growth.

God, in His wisdom, led me on a path of learning patience. It was a challenging process that required me to dig deep and uproot the negative traits that had been holding me back. I had to confront the fact that my impatience was a result of being spoiled and not being taught the value of waiting. It was a characteristic that had been reinforced by my family, friends, and even romantic partners.

I vividly remember a moment when someone challenged my entitlement and asked, "Who do you think you are?" This encounter shook me to my core and made me realize the extent of my impatience. Instead of responding with grace and understanding, I sought validation from others and used them to fill the void of being told no. It was a destructive pattern that I had to break free from.

God used various experiences to help me overcome my selfishness and impatience. I had to catch my mind when it started to dwell on thoughts of entitlement and dissatisfaction. I learned to bring every thought captive to the obedience of Christ and to focus on gratitude for what I already had. This shift in mindset allowed me to appreciate the present moment and find contentment amid waiting.

Practicing patience also required me to exercise discipline and self-control. I forced myself to wait even when I didn't want to, embracing the uncomfortable and accepting that things don't always go according to my timeline. I learned to behave with grace and humility while waiting, rather than pouting, complaining, or whining. As Joyce Meyer once said, "Patience is not simply the ability to wait—it's how we behave while we're waiting."

Through this journey, I have experienced the transformative power of patience. It has taught me the importance of surrendering control and trusting in God's timing. It has allowed me to develop a greater sense of self-discipline and a deeper appreciation for the blessings in my life. Patience has become a guiding principle in my interactions with others and has brought a sense of peace and fulfillment that I had never experienced before.

I'd pray this daily:

Heavenly Father, Your Word is a lamp to my feet and a light to my path. Your Word teaches me wisdom and fills me with newness of life. As I come to you today, I bring my needs to you. Help me to lay down all my problems at your feet. Help me to lay down all my tangled thoughts and restless emotions. Lord, I am seeking your peace and your patience. I want to learn to wait patiently for you to bring your answers to my prayers. I want to cooperate with your plans for me. Thank you for assuring me that your

*plans for me are good. As I wait on you, I will continue to turn
to your Word for comfort and direction. Your Word is solid and
reliable. Your Word steadies me. Your Word brings me truth. Your
Word gives me strength. Your Word chases away my worry and
my fears. Your Word refreshes me.*
    Thank you for your Word. Amen

Learning to be patient was not only a lesson in dealing with other people, but it also required me to trust God and have patience towards Him. I had to let go of my need for control and accept that there are situations in life that I have no control over. It was a humbling experience that taught me to rely on God's timing and wisdom.

One scripture that became a source of comfort and guidance for me was Psalm 40:31, which says, "But those who wait for the LORD shall renew their strength; they shall mount up with wings like eagles; they shall run and not be weary; they shall walk and not faint." This verse reminded me that when I patiently wait on the Lord, He will give me the strength I need to endure and overcome any challenges that come my way.

Another scripture that resonated with me was Romans 2:7, which states, "To those who by patience in well-doing seek for glory and honor and immortality, he will give eternal life." This verse highlights the importance of patience in our pursuit of righteousness and eternal life. It reminded me that patience is not just a virtue to be practiced in earthly matters, but it also has eternal significance.

Patience is closely linked to humility and is the antithesis of pride. Ecclesiastes 7:8 tells us that the patient in spirit is better than the proud in spirit. This verse emphasizes the importance of cultivating a patient and humble attitude, recognizing that we are not in control and that God's timing is perfect.

Patience is not something that comes naturally to us; it requires faith. Hebrews 6:12 encourages us to be imitators of those who through faith and patience inherit the promises. Patience is a product of our faith in God's faithfulness and His promises. It is through faith that we can endure and wait with hope, even when we cannot see the fulfillment of our desires.

Part of our spiritual growth and maturity is learning to discern the difference between a denial and a delay. Sometimes, God's answer to our prayers may be "no" or "not yet." Hebrews 10:37 reminds us that God will come and will not delay, but His timing may not align with our own. It is during these times of delay that our patience is tested and refined. God uses these delays to strengthen our faith, deepen our trust in Him, and reveal our level of commitment.

When we are tempted to lose patience with God, it is important to remember how patient He has been with us. God's patience and faithfulness towards us are immeasurable. He has shown us grace and mercy time and time again, even when we fall short. Reflecting on His patience can inspire us to extend the same patience toward Him, knowing that His plans are perfect, and His timing is always right.

Prayer

Heavenly Father, help me develop the fruit of patience in every area of my life, especially dealing with the little annoyances that get me frustrated. Help me overcome my feelings of anger or impatience so that I can look at things with peace, joy, love, and hope. Amen.

COMPONENT 5
OBEDIENCE

Psalm 128:1
"Blessed are all who fear the LORD,
who walk in obedience to him."

Obedience is a concept that holds great power and significance in our relationship with God. It is the act of complying with God's commands, submitting to His authority, and demonstrating our love and faithfulness to Him. While obedience may seem simple in theory, it can be challenging to put into practice due to our inherent imperfections and the temptations of the world.

In John 14:15, Jesus clearly states, "If you love me, you will obey what I command." This concise statement encapsulates the essence of obedience. It serves as a reminder that our obedience to God reflects our love for Him. When we truly love God, we will naturally desire to follow His commands and live per His will.

However, obedience is not always easy. Our human nature often leads us astray, causing us to prioritize our desires and interests over God's commands. We are prone to sin and temptation, which can make it difficult to consistently obey God's laws. It requires self-discipline, self-control, and a constant reliance on God's strength and guidance.

Yet, despite the challenges, obedience to God is crucial for our spiritual growth and well-being. It is through our obedience that we demonstrate our faithfulness to Him and deepen our relationship with Him. In 1 John 2:3-6, it is emphasized that those who claim to know God must walk in obedience to His commands. Obedience is not just a mere act of compliance; it is a way of life that reflects our commitment to following Jesus and living out His teachings.

Obedience to God is not solely motivated by fear or a sense of obligation. It is driven by love and a desire to honor and please Him. In 1 John 5:2-3, it is stated that loving God means keeping His commands, and His commands are not burdensome. Obedience is not meant to be a heavy burden, but rather a joyful response to God's love and grace. It is a way for us to align our lives with His perfect plan and experience the abundant life He has promised us.

Prayer plays a vital role in our journey of obedience. Through prayer, we can seek God's guidance, ask for His strength to overcome temptation, and express our willingness to obey His commands. Prayer allows us to surrender our own will and align ourselves with God's will, inviting Him to work in and through us.

My Prayer:

Heavenly Father, today I begin by thanking you for your amazing grace. Thank you, Lord, for the way your grace has filled, shaped, and guided my life. Thank you for the privilege of living in your grace each day. May I seek to obey you in all that I do, Lord, not to earn your favor, but so that I might respond appropriately to your favor already given to me. As I receive your mercies, which are new every morning, may they motivate me to offer myself to you, all that I am, all that I do. May my obedience to you be an act of thanksgiving, a demonstration of my love for you. All praise be to you, Lord, because you have rescued me from sin and death and because your grace fills my life each day. Amen.

As we navigate through the challenges and hardships of life, it is important to look to the examples of those who have endured suffering with faith. These individuals serve as a reminder that even in sorrow and pain, we can find strength and purpose in our obedience to God. It is tempting to become discouraged and forsake our service to the Lord when faced with difficult circumstances, but doing so would mean missing out on the valuable lessons that obedience can teach us.

Suffering can be an opportunity for growth and spiritual maturity. Each time we experience suffering, it presents a chance for us to learn obedience through the things we endure. It is through these trials that we can develop a deeper understanding of God's faithfulness and our reliance on Him. Rather than allowing suffering to discourage us, we should use it as a catalyst for reflection and a reminder of the solid and secure foundation we have in Christ.

However, obedience is not always easy, especially when our desires conflict with what God calls us to do. The desires of the flesh and the temptations of the world can be powerful forces that pull us away from obedience. It is in these moments that we must rely on God's strength and guidance to overcome the negative influences and choose obedience.

I struggled with obedience, particularly in how I responded to my pain and suffering. Instead of turning to God and seeking His comfort and guidance, I chose to self-medicate and engage in disobedient actions. I knew deep down that what I was doing was wrong, and I felt convicted each time I acted out. It was a clear example of the battle between my free will and the call to obedience.

In Hebrews 5:8, it is stated that Jesus learned obedience through what He suffered. This verse reminds us that even Jesus, the Son of God, experienced suffering and had to learn obedience. It is a reminder that obedience is a lifelong journey of growth and learning and that even in our imperfections, we can strive to be obedient to God's will.

Ultimately, obedience is a choice that we have the power to make. God has given us free will, and it is up to us to choose obedience over disobedience. It may not always be easy, and we may stumble along the way, but with God's grace and guidance, we can press on and lay up treasure in heaven. In the eternal kingdom, there will be no more suffering, pain, or tears, and all things will be made new. May we strive to be obedient to God's commands, even in the face of adversity, knowing that our obedience is a testament to our love and faithfulness to Him.

Prayer

Heavenly Father, you are the Lord of Lords and the King of Kings. You are the beginning and end, the Being over all authorities. Today I come to You with a humble heart. I admit that I make myself the Lord of my life at times and for that.

Thank You, Lord, for constantly knocking on my heart. For opening my eyes to see that I cannot continue living my life on my terms. Thank you for reminding me that I must first and foremost obey you and your commands if I want to live an abundant life. Thank you that even though I fall short in obedience, you continue to love me and pursue my heart.

Remove the stubbornness in my heart and fill it with your unconditional love so there would be no room for me to disobey. I ask that you give me a humble and repentant heart on days when I do not feel like obeying you. I understand that half-obedience is still disobedience. So, Father, change my heart from the inside out and give me strength and wisdom to follow You wholeheartedly. It is in your matchless name I pray. Amen.

COMPONENT 6
TRUST

Proverbs 3:5-6
Trust in the Lord with all your heart and lean not
on your own understanding; in all your ways submit to him,
and he will make your paths straight

Trust—firm belief in the reliability, truth, ability, or strength of someone or something.

Learning to trust takes time and patience, something that I lacked in the past. I found myself caught in a cycle of impatience, desperately seeking relief from the pressures and stresses of life. However, it was through the process of learning patience that God began to cultivate trust within me.

Trusting was not easy for me, especially considering the turmoil that had consumed my life. I had experienced so much pain and disappointment that I found it difficult to trust anyone, including God. This lack of trust led me to a miserable and paranoid existence. I constantly worried about everything, looking over my shoulder and taking matters into my own hands. I made choices and decisions without seeking guidance, only to find myself in even more pain.

It was a simple concept, yet incredibly challenging to put into practice—learning to trust God over myself. When faced with adversity, my initial reaction was not to turn to the Lord for salvation. I was living in bondage and fear, unable to break free from the cycle of self-reliance. I realized that the coping mechanisms I had relied on in the past were no longer serving me. They were keeping me from experiencing true joy and preventing me from receiving help and support from others.

I had convinced myself that I needed to protect myself and rely solely on my strength to stay safe. But those emotional self-protection strategies were only hurting me and keeping me captive. I was in survival mode, unaware that God was with me in those darkest moments. I didn't see Him physically present in the rooms where I was abused and violated, but I now understand that His presence was there because I am still here today.

In John 15:5, Jesus reminds us that apart from Him, we can do nothing. This verse serves as a powerful reminder that we need to lean on Him for help in every aspect of our lives. It is through trusting in Him that we can find true healing and freedom.

Through my journey of learning to trust, I have come to realize that God uses the challenges and hardships we face to shape us into who He intends us to be. Even when we cannot see Him physically, He is always there, working behind the scenes for our good. It is through patience, surrender, and a willingness to trust that we can experience the transformative power of God's love and faithfulness.

When I meditate on Proverbs 3:5-6, it serves as a powerful reminder of the fundamental role trust plays in our relationship with God. Trust is the very first word mentioned in this scripture, emphasizing its significance in our faith journey. Without trust, we cannot fully embrace and follow the rest of God's command.

In my own life, I have experienced the consequences of relying on my understanding rather than trusting in God. When I solely depended on my limited perspective and reasoning, I made irrational decisions and convinced myself that God was not by my side. I fell into the trap of believing that I needed to protect myself and take control of my circumstances.

However, I have come to realize that when we rely on our understanding, we distance ourselves from God. We become imbalanced and lose sight of His sovereignty. I vividly recall a time in my past relationship when I struggled to comprehend why God was saying "no" to my desire to remain with my ex-husband. I mistakenly believed that losing him meant losing something valuable, when in reality, God knew that continuing in that relationship would only lead to more heartbreak. My perception was clouded by my desires and limited understanding.

Trusting in the Lord with all our hearts means that we cannot prioritize our own need for understanding above His right to direct our lives as He sees fit. Insisting on God always making sense to us sets us up for spiritual trouble. We must acknowledge that we cannot fully grasp all that God is doing in our lives, but we must still trust and embrace His plans.

Trusting God can be challenging because we can only see what is directly in front of us. We may find ourselves in difficult situations, such as emotionally or mentally abusive relationships, and wonder why God doesn't provide an immediate way out. However, often there are valuable lessons to be learned or character traits that God is refining within us. Trusting God means having faith that He has our best interests at heart, even when we struggle to understand His ways.

Learning to trust God requires us to let go of our self-reliance and need for self-protection. It is a process of seeking wisdom and understanding from God's Word. As we delve into the Bible and engage in Bible studies, we gain clarity and insight into God's principles and laws. Applying these principles to our lives can bring about transformation and change.

We must always remember that God possesses infinite wisdom, and His ways surpass our own. Romans 11:33 reminds us of the depth and richness of God's wisdom, which is beyond our comprehension. Every day, we must consciously surrender our plans and expectations to His plans, trusting that His wisdom far exceeds our own.

Trust in God is not only crucial for our spiritual growth but also for our overall well-being. It requires us to release our understanding and lean on His wisdom and guidance. Trusting God means surrendering our plans and expectations to His plans, even when they don't align with our desires. May we continually seek wisdom and understanding from God's Word and trust in His sovereignty in every aspect of our lives.

Prayer

Heavenly Father, help me trust you with my decisions and future. Let me lean on you with all my heart instead of relying on my own imperfect understanding. Give me clear guidance in my life. I ask for your help to direct my path. Father, I struggle to trust others, so it's no wonder I am unsure of my trust in You at times. Forgive me and grow me. Teach me to trust your direction. Help me to have confidence in your guidance. Turn my life into a powerful demonstration of what trust in God looks like. I ask this in your matchless name, Amen.

COMPONENT 7

LOVE

1 Corinthians 13:13
And now these three remain: faith, hope and love.
But the greatest of these is love.

Love is a complex and multifaceted concept that can be seen in various forms and understood differently depending on the context and the object of our affection. The dictionary defines love as an intense feeling of deep affection, and while this definition captures a part of its essence, it falls short of encompassing the true depth and meaning of love.

From a biblical perspective, love is not merely a feeling, but a purposeful commitment to sacrificial action for the well-being of another. It is a selfless and unconditional love that goes beyond emotions and desires. In 1 John 4:8, it is stated that God is love, highlighting the central role that love plays in our lives and our relationship with God.

Different types of love are described in the Bible. One of them is "*Agape*," which is often referred to as God's divine love. Agape is characterized by its unconditional nature and sacrificial commitment. It is the love that motivated God to sacrifice His Son for the salvation of humanity, and it is the love that Jesus demonstrated by willingly laying down His life for us. Agape love puts the well-being of others above our own, even to the point of self-sacrifice.

Another type of love is "*Phileo*," which is often described as brotherly or friendship love. It is a love that is based on mutual affection and shared experiences. Phileo love is characterized by a deep bond and a sense of camaraderie. It is the love that exists between close friends and family members.

"*Eros*" is another type of love that is often associated with romantic and passionate love. It is a love that is felt within the body and is driven by deep and beautiful procreative urges. While Eros is intimately connected to sexual desire, it is not limited to it. Eros can also be experienced in deeply intimate friendships and can lead to the creation of families and lasting joy.

While all these types of love are important and can coexist, Agape love stands out as the highest form of love. It is a love that is free from the limitations and errors of our human nature. Agape love is the glue that holds the other loves together and provides us with the wisdom and patience to navigate the complexities of relationships when the other forms of love fail.

LOVING GOD

Deuteronomy 11:13, "So if you faithfully obey the commands I am giving you today —to love the Lord your God and to serve him with all your heart and with all your soul."

Mark 12:30, "And you shall love the Lord your God with all your heart, and with all your soul, and with all your mind, and with all your strength. It may appear simple, but we first have to understand our heart. What is the heart and what is its purpose?

Our hearts are more than an organ that pumps blood. It's more than the seat of our emotions; it's compounded of emotions but also of our mind, our will, and our conscience. So basically, our heart is the source of our feelings, thoughts, intentions, and our sense of condemnation or guilt. Don't get it confused with our soul; our soul is also made up of our emotions and our will; the psychological part of our person. There is a subtle difference otherwise he wouldn't say, "Love me with all your heart and soul" he'd use one or the other. *Hebrews 4:12, "For the word of God is* *living and active, sharper than any two-edged sword, piercing to the division of soul and of spirit, of joints and of marrow, and discerning the thoughts and intentions of the heart."* The Lord created us with a heart so that we would love Him. *1 John 4:19, "God first loved us in that He infused us with His love and generated within us the love with which we love Him and the brothers."*

To love God with all your heart means we must know that our affections determine our devotion. Our hearts are full of affection and desires. Our affections are deep waves that navigate our lives. To determine where our affections lie, we must determine what occupies our time and what motivates our actions.

We must understand that our affections follow what we treasure. Matthew 6:21, "For where your treasure is, there your heart will also be." The heart loves what it treasures! Matthew 13:44, "The kingdom of heavens is like treasure hidden in a field. When a man found it, he hid it again, and then in his joy, went and sold all he had and bought that field." To love God completely we must treasure him supremely. When we truly encounter the Lord in His glory and worth, loving Him with all our hearts will be easy.

We must also spend time with the Lord and let his light shine in our hearts. 2 Corinthians 4:6-7, "For God, who said, "Let light shine out of darkness," made his light shine in our hearts to give us the light of the knowledge of the glory God in the face of Christ. But we have this treasure in jars of clay to show that this all-surpassing power is from God and not from us."

Our soul, as I said previously, is our mind, emotion, and will. God created our soul so we could express Him, however, because of the fall, we tend to express ourselves. We give our own opinions, our feelings, and our own decisions apart from God. Our soul is an imperishable thing. When we die our soul remains but exits the body. I've heard it been said that only two things last: the Word of God and the souls of men.

Our mind is the leading part of our soul, directing the rest of our being. It can be set on many things, but God intended it to be set on the spirit, where Christ is. *Romans 8:6, "For the mind set on the flesh is death, but the mind set on the spirit is life and peace."* By setting our mind on our spirit, our whole being is focused on God. We can set our minds on the spirit by reading the bible with an open heart. As we read, our mind is enlightened and renewed. Reading God's word daily greatly benefits our minds and our entire soul.

Our strength refers to our physical strength. When we turn our hearts to the Lord, express Him in our soul, and set our mind on Him, our body will follow. As love for the Lord permeates all our inward parts, our outward actions begin to change. Things that used to occupy our time and energy will give way because what we love has changed.

Oh, my goodness, I can go on for days talking about love. I'll try to compact it a little; I'll try but no guarantees.

SELF LOVE

Self-love, we can only love others as much as we love ourselves. Mark 12:31, "…The second is this; Love your neighbor as you love yourself." There is no commandment greater than these."

Romans 12:3, "For by the grace given me I say to every one of you; Do not think of yourself more highly than you ought, but rather think of yourself with sober judgment, in accordance with the faith God has distributed to each of you."

Practicing self-love involves learning how to trust ourselves, treat ourselves with respect, and be kind and affectionate towards ourselves. Cultivating self-love and self-acceptance is not optional. They are a priority as well. Self-love is important to living well. Self-love is not makeover or new clothes, although they feel good and are gratifying, you can't grow or buy self-love. We cultivate love when we allow our most vulnerable and powerful selves to be deeply seen and known and when we honor the spiritual connection that grows from that offering with trust, respect, kindness, and affection. It's not something we give or get; it is something that we nurture and grow. It can only be cultivated between two people when it exists within each one of us.

I struggled with self-love for a while. I blamed myself for all the terrible things that were done to me. I know it may be hard to understand how I could love God so much and be so grounded in love yet struggled with self-love. It seems so contradicting. Honestly, I didn't view them as the same, I didn't see myself as God seen me. I didn't feel worthy, and I had self-esteem issues. I had to determine that whatever had been done in the past, I could not let it affect the way I shaped my future. It was holding on to all the terrible things from my past that made me feel unworthy. In *2 Corinthians 5:17*, it states, *"Therefore, if anyone is in Christ, the new creation has come: The old has gone, the new is hear."* A friend of mine said something simple but powerful and it resonated in my spirit deeply. She said, "If you have given your life to Him, you are a new creation, why are you spending time wearing the sins of the old; even if you weren't the one sinning?" After that, I looked at that scripture differently and I changed my clothes. All she did was use the word.

It took a lot of prayer for self-love to manifest:

Lord, help me to see myself the way you see me. Thank you that you see me through your eyes of love and all you created me to be. Enable me to open my heart to receive your love. Although it's hard to comprehend a love so great, and I don't feel worthy of it, I don't want to shut myself off from the power of your amazing love working in my heart. Teach me about the ways you love me that I do not understand. Give me eyes to see how you reveal your love for me by keeping me from things that are not your greatest good for my life. I know that everything you want to do in my life cannot be accomplished without your love flowing into me.

Help me turn my gaze from myself to you. I want to see you more clearly and understand you more fully. Thank you that you not only love me, but you will enable me to understand the depth of your love. Show me the ways I don't recognize or open to your love, whether because of serious doubt or simply a lack of understanding, and I have missed many of your blessings because of it.

Enable me to see my life from your perspective, instead of looking through a magnifying lens to see the flaws in myself, help me to see the good and potential for greatness you have put in me. May your presence be magnified in my life beyond what I can even imagine. Cause our perfection, beauty, love, and holiness are to be always reflected in me. In Jesus name, I pray. Amen!

Lord, thank you that you love me and that you made me for your purpose. Help me to appreciate all you have put in me. Enable me to recognize the gifts you have given me to be used for your glory. Enable me to see the good I'm not seeing and reject the self-criticism I focus on. Teach me to love you more and love myself better so I can express love to others with greater clarity.

I confess any feelings I have about my life that are negative and critical. You oversee my life, and I trust you to bring good into it. Give me wisdom to see the great things you have put in my life that will be used for your glory. Help me to love others as you have taught me to love myself—that is, with great appreciation for your work in me and in them. I know that when I love you, myself, and others this is the fulfillment of the law.

Help me to pursue righteousness, godliness, faith, love, patience, and gentleness, because they are beautiful in your eyes and pleasing to you. Lord, you are beautiful and wonderful and lovely and attractive and desirable. Let all that you are shine through all that I am. Help me to love myself in a way that doesn't say "I am great," but rather says, "You are great! And you are in me making me more like you every day." In Jesus name, I pray. Amen!

It wasn't until after my divorce that I began the innermost process of self-discovery. I had placed so much of the expectation that my husband would provide me with the love I needed. I was so caught up waiting for him to love me that I had forgotten about the one person I needed to love first—Me.

I studied love daily, the love of God, the love of many successful relationships, the love of many broken relationships, how to apply it in every relationship I encountered, love for people who treated me poorly, those who I felt didn't even deserve my love. I began practicing it, journaling about it, and speaking about it. I wrote pages and pages about love. I had become enamored by it, enamored by God; his love for me.

Aside from lots of prayer, I set boundaries for myself and others, protecting my heart, and my ears; I was careful who and what I listened to and my eyes; I was careful what I watched and who I was around. I wrote down what I liked about myself and what I disliked. I took each thing, one by one and I increased what I liked and worked to change the things I did not like. I alternated so that I wasn't consistently dealing with the bad or fooling myself that everything was all good.

Most of us, if not all of us know *1 Corinthians 13:1-7, "Love is patient, love is kind. It does not envy, it does not boast, it is not proud. It does not dishonor others, it is not self-seeking, it is not easily angered, it keeps no record of wrongs. Love does not delight in evil but rejoices with the truth. It always protects, always trust, always hopes, always perseveres. Love never fails..."*

Love is patient—(long-suffering) Love bears pain or trials without complaint, and is steadfast despite opposition, difficulty, or adversity.

Love is kind—Love is sympathetic, considerate, gentle, and agreeable.

Love is not jealous—Love does not participate in rivalry, is not hostile towards one believed to enjoy an advantage, and is not suspicious.

Love does not brag—Love does not flaunt itself boastfully and does not engage in self-glorification.

Love is not arrogant—Even when you think you are right. Love does not assert itself or become overbearing in dealing with others.

Love does not act unbecomingly—Love does not behave seemly.

Love does not seek its own—Biblical love is not selfish and self-seeking.

Love is not provoked—Love is not aroused or incited to outbursts of anger, even if others attempt to provoke you.

Love does not consider a wrong suffered—Love does not hold a grudge. Love forgives, chooses not to bring up past wrongs in accusation or retaliation, and does not return evil for evil. Love covers a multitude of sins.

Love does not rejoice in unrighteousness—Love mourns over sin, its effects, and the pain that results from living in a fallen world. Love seeks to reconcile others with the Lord.

Love rejoices with the truth—Love is joyful when the truth is known, even when it may lead to adverse circumstances, reviling, and persecution.

Love bears all things—Love is tolerant, and endures with others who are difficult to understand or deal with. Love remembers that God develops spiritual maturity through difficult circumstances.

Love believes all things—Love accepts trustfully, does not judge people's motives, and believes others until facts prove otherwise.

Love hopes all things—Love expects fulfillment of God's plan and anticipates the best for the other person. Love confidently entrusts others to the Lord to do His sovereign and perfect will in their lives.

Love endures all things—Love remains steadfast under suffering or hardship without yielding and returns good while undergoing trials.

Love never fails—Love will not crumble under pressure or difficulties. Love remains selflessly faithful even to the point of death.

Even through all the hell I've been through, I am grateful that I was grounded in love to the extent that I was. Despite it all, I never have, and I never will give up on love.

Prayer

Heavenly Father, help me to love how you love. Amen

4
HEALED

Psalm 147:3
He heals the brokenhearted and binds up their wounds

After experiencing the transformative process of healing guided by God, I now embrace a life liberated from the chains of bondage and the grip of strongholds that once consumed me. This newfound freedom allows me to live with a renewed sense of purpose, joy, and inner peace, unburdened by the past and empowered to embrace the present and future with hope and resilience.

It's important to understand that healing is a continuous process that requires ongoing effort. The enemy will always try to bring back negative thoughts and memories, which is why it's crucial to live according to the word of God. So, when I say that I'm healed, it doesn't mean that those thoughts never come back. It simply means that I've embarked on a journey from a place of torment to a place of joy. I am no longer questioning why I'm not in anguish over past experiences, which for me means I've healed. "I want to be transparent about something—sometimes I still struggle with depression and anxiety. However, I have learned some helpful tools to manage those feelings when they arise. It's not that they disappear completely, but I have learned how to handle them when they come up. That looks like healing to me.

Throughout this process, I have found solace and strength in various sources, including my faith in God, the power of prayer, the support of my loved ones, the aid of medication, the therapeutic outlet of writing, the healing influence of music, and the unwavering love and presence of my children and family. These combined forces have been instrumental in guiding me toward a path of healing, resilience, and personal growth. Another source that was very helpful for me was, I told you all about the greeting cards I made and shared with my mother when she was in transition. Those cards I would mail to myself. It may seem weird, but that was a form of encouraging myself and let me tell you not knowing when those cards would arrive but arriving right on time when I needed them was profound.

In addition to prioritizing my mental and emotional well-being, I have also learned to handle rejection and control my anger. I no longer react impulsively or with aggression when faced with a "no." Instead, I approach these situations with humility, understanding that rejection does not define my worth. It is both humbling and amusing to hear stories from my family and friends about the person I used to be, a mess that they fervently prayed for God to intervene in. I am grateful for their support and apologize for the sleepless nights I may have caused them. The tears I have shed throughout my journey have been plentiful, but I recognize that it is through God's intervention and grace that I have been able to overcome.

Through consistent prayer and relying on God, I have successfully eliminated unhealthy desires from my life. This shift in focus has brought about a profound sense of peace, not only mentally but also physically. It has enabled me to cultivate self-love and appreciation, seeing myself in a new light and desiring to be noticed by others in a way that aligns with my true identity. This journey of self-discovery has made me emerge as a stronger and more authentic version of myself, embracing the woman I was always meant to be.

I am committed to resisting the temptations that arise each day. Every morning, I equip myself with the Armor of God, preparing for any challenges that may come my way. Singing songs of praise and expressing gratitude for God's blessings and His presence in my life brings me solace and strength. It is my priority to cast down any negative thoughts or imaginations that contradict the knowledge of God. I strive to align every thought with the obedience of Christ, as stated in 2 Corinthians 10:5.

My journey of healing and self-discovery has led me to a place of freedom, purpose, and inner peace. I have learned to accept and address my struggles, finding strength in various sources of support. By prioritizing my mental and emotional well-being, handling rejection with humility, seeking solace in God, and resisting temptations, I have experienced profound personal growth and emerged as a more authentic version of myself. I am grateful for the transformative power of God's love and grace in my life.

Being unhealed had significant consequences in my life, costing me precious time, missed opportunities, and strained relationships. I can't even begin to count the number of sleepless nights I endured due to my emotional instability. I realized that I had placed unrealistic expectations on others, expecting them to understand and cater to my needs, even though I hadn't fully acknowledged or addressed them myself. I felt entitled to constant affirmation and validation from others, believing that my past hardships warranted special treatment, even though many people were unaware of the struggles I had faced.

My lack of trust in others was pervasive, extending to almost everyone I encountered. I struggled to discern whether someone had ill intentions toward me or if it was simply my fear and insecurity clouding my judgment. This lack of discernment led to detrimental behaviors, such as accusing others without valid reasons and crying foul when faced with competition or perceived mistreatment. These behaviors ultimately sabotaged my chances of success, as evidenced by the missed opportunity to work for a District Attorney's office. Despite being the top candidate, my emotional outbursts and unfounded accusations led to their decision not to select me.

Similar patterns emerged in other job applications and relationships. Upon hearing that other candidates were being considered, I internalized it as a personal attack and reacted with intense emotions. I wrote letters and made phone calls, creating unnecessary drama and further damaging my chances of success. These experiences highlight the detrimental impact of my unhealed state on my professional and personal life.

In my relationships, I noticed that I was displaying unhealthy behavior. I used to accuse others of actions they may or may not have done, projecting my insecurities onto them. However, this does not mean that they were responsible for my behavior. I realized that I had to own up to my mistakes. This constant pattern of accusation and emotional outbursts took a toll on the people around me, causing strained relationships and, in some cases, leading to their end. I am grateful to have had loving people in my life who understood and forgave me, giving me the chance to rebuild and strengthen broken relationships. However, I also recognize that some people were not meant to be a part of my journey, as they did not align with God's plan for me.

Upon reflecting on my experiences, I have become aware of the destructive impact of my unhealed state. I now understand the importance of addressing my emotional wounds and being responsible for my actions and reactions. I am committed to seeking healing and growth to become a healthier version of myself. This will enable me to navigate relationships and opportunities with grace, discernment, and emotional stability. I am grateful for the lessons I have learned and the opportunity to rebuild and nurture the relationships that truly matter in my life.

When you begin the process of healing, you will adopt a new way of talking to yourself. You'll offer yourself more understanding, support, and love while being less judgmental and shameful. Over time, you will start feeling a greater sense of belonging and inner peace. Your self-confidence will return, allowing you to make life decisions with more certainty and without guilt or self-doubt. Looking back on situations will no longer overwhelm you with emotion. If you're struggling with any form of abuse, past or present, I encourage you to seek help and turn to the word of God for guidance and support. While the matchless power of God is sufficient, you must also put in the work, as faith without work doesn't work. Although it's hard work, the other side of the journey is filled with happiness and joy. With God, anything within his will is possible.

Prayer

Heavenly Father, I am grateful for your healing power, and for the abundant blessings you have given me. You omnipotent and eternal God, I give you all the praise and glory. Without you within me, I am nothing.

Amen.

5
HEALED AGAIN

After feeling like my healing journey was finally stabilizing, I was met with another setback that completely shook me to my core. In March 2020, amidst battling COVID-19, I received the devastating news that I also had gastric cancer, the same type that took my mother's life in 2012. The overwhelming fear I experienced made me imagine a similar fate.

With my condition, it was determined that chemotherapy would be the most suitable course of action. However, the mere thought of undergoing this treatment filled me with an unprecedented fear. The shadow of my mother's battle with the same cancer loomed over me, as she tragically lost her life to it. I couldn't help but connect her story to mine, creating a deeply distressing situation. My mind and emotions were thrown into turmoil, as I grappled with the fear and uncertainty that accompanied my journey. It's important to know that in battle, especially similar battles, we do not take on other journeys. I had to understand that her journey was not mine and had to fight it from that perspective no matter what it looked like.

Despite undergoing chemotherapy and successfully beating cancer, the constant mental battle persisted, especially when I had a slight stomachache. While I try to remind myself that her story is hers and mine is mine, there are moments when the human part of me wonders. However, amidst the doubts and fears, I choose to trust and believe in my journey. I recognize that each person's experience with cancer is unique, and I am determined to fight and overcome any obstacles that come my way. It serves as a constant reminder to cherish every moment, find strength in resilience, and hold onto hope for a brighter tomorrow.

Fortunately, my cancer was detected in its early stages, giving me a significant advantage in my battle against it. However, there was a delay in starting treatment due to the complexities of finding a safe approach that wouldn't compromise my health, especially considering the presence of COVID-19 in my body. This gap in treatment was challenging, as I experienced severe symptoms and had to endure multiple hospital visits.

During this time, my fever would spike to alarming levels, reaching 104 degrees at times. The intensity of the fever made me fear the worst, as it felt like my body was being pushed to its limits. The excruciating pain and high fever made me worry about the potential loss of my legs; it took a major toll on me.

The back-and-forth visits to the hospital became a regular part of my life, as medical professionals worked tirelessly to monitor my condition and provide the necessary care.

Again, prayer became my lifeline during this challenging period. I turned to my faith, seeking solace and guidance in moments of despair. Through countless prayers, I found the strength to maintain my sanity and hold onto hope. It was through this spiritual connection that I discovered the power to navigate the overwhelming emotions and uncertainties that accompanied my illness.

As I embarked on my chemotherapy journey, the physical toll became evident as I started losing weight rapidly, shedding around 30 pounds. The most visible change, however, was the loss of my hair. While some may argue that our hair does not define us, I couldn't help but feel its absence deeply. Seeing myself in the mirror without my familiar long hair was a constant reminder of the impact cancer had on my appearance. Night after night, I would go to bed only to wake up to clumps of hair scattered on my pillow. I would gather them up, tears streaming down my face, and store them in a sandwich bag. This ritual continued for several days, and even in the shower, my hair would fall out in handfuls. Running my fingers through my hair became a painful experience as more and more strands would come loose. It was a heartbreaking process.

A dear friend, who also happened to be my hairdresser, eventually intervened. She gently advised me to let go and cut off all my hair. She assured me that it would grow back, but continuing to witness the hair loss day after day was only tormenting me unnecessarily. So, one morning, I decided to take matters into my own hands. I stood inside the shower, leaning against the wall, and mustered the courage to say goodbye to the old version of myself. With a prayer in my heart, I grabbed a chair, positioned it in front of the mirror, and shaved off all my hair.

The range of emotions I experienced during this process was overwhelming. I felt hurt, angry, discouraged, and surprisingly, even joyful. I was angry at the situation, resentful that I had to let go of my hair. I feared how I would look and who I would become, despite knowing deep down that my hair did not define my identity. I also felt joyous, relieved that I would no longer find strands of hair on my pillow or the shower floor.

After the drastic haircut, I couldn't bring myself to look at my reflection for a while. I knew what I would see, but I wasn't ready to truly face it. It took until the next day for me to gather the courage to gaze at myself in the mirror for an extended period. I encouraged myself, reminding myself that this was a necessary step in my journey. I took it day by day, capturing some pictures along the way.

Acceptance didn't come easy, but it arrived sooner than I expected. I cried every day for a couple of weeks, mourning the loss of my hair, but eventually, I found the strength to move forward. It was a difficult adjustment, as I looked and felt like a completely different person.

Despite the support and love I received from those around me, there was still a sense of loneliness in my experience. While countless messages of encouragement flooded in, there was a part of me that resisted them. In a moment, I felt that the encouragement was preventing me from fully embracing my true emotions of sadness, hurt, and discouragement. It was a complex mix of gratitude for the support and a need to honor my feelings authentically.

After a decade of dedicated work as an investigator, I made the difficult decision to take a leave of absence from my job. In my line of work, being sharp and focused was crucial, but I found myself unable to concentrate. The task of interviewing numerous individuals, and hearing their stories while grappling with my own, became overwhelming. It provided a unique perspective, reminding me of the importance of prioritizing my own needs during this challenging time. I realized that I couldn't give my all to my job because I needed to reserve that energy for myself. Balancing a demanding workload, battling illnesses, being a mother, and simply living became an impossible feat. Adding to the complexity, I was still fighting the lingering effects of COVID-19, which had taken a toll on my mental acuity. I knew I wasn't as sharp as I used to be, whether due to the virus, cancer, or a combination of both. This realization weighed heavily on my emotions.

I had to make a difficult decision about my job. Staying on would have made things worse for me and the people I worked for.

Family holds immense importance in my life, but due to my treatment and the ongoing concerns surrounding COVID-19, I was unable to see them for months. The emotional toll this took on me was significant. I found myself seeking solace in the shower, where I would often cry for extended periods. Thankfully, technology allowed me to connect with my family through FaceTime, but I consciously chose not to do so as frequently as I should have. Why? Because I knew that seeing me in my weakened state would only break their hearts further. While not being able to have them physically present was beyond my control, I decided to limit phone conversations. Additionally, my persistent cough made it difficult to engage in any conversation without triggering a coughing fit, which left me feeling drained. I spent days pouring my heart out to the Lord, feeling helpless and finding comfort only in prayer and the word.

The experience of being separated from my family was tremendously difficult. As a mother, my children have always held a special place in my heart, and it was tough knowing that they were worried and scared for me. The uncertainty of whether I would make it through each day, combined with the fact that I couldn't have them with me, only made their concerns worse. I wanted to mention these challenges because my illness didn't just affect me, it also impacted the lives of all my loved ones and friends. The weight of everything was heavy on my heart and mind.

By March 2021, a year into my diagnosis, I began to feel some improvement. COVID-19 still lingered, but my health was gradually improving. I had completed my chemotherapy treatments and started to notice a slight fuzz on my scalp. Although my appetite was still not fully restored, I tried to consume smoothies and protein drinks, working towards regaining my strength.

March 2022 will forever be etched in my memory as the day I rang the bell, declaring my victory over cancer. As I drove to my appointment, nervous excitement filled my mind. To calm my racing thoughts, I decided to stop and grab some oatmeal, giving myself an hour to collect myself before the appointment. Sitting in the parking lot, I listened to music and offered up prayers, seeking strength and reassurance.

When it was time to finally enter the clinic, my feet felt heavy. I was called back for a final blood draw, and the wait for the results felt like an eternity. The smiles on my nurses' faces gave me a glimmer of hope, but I didn't want to assume anything. Finally, I was called into the doctor's office, where he went over my numbers. He started with the high cholesterol, a common side effect of the medications I was on, before revealing the other numbers. I couldn't quite decipher the significance, so I mustered the courage to ask him directly, "Can you just tell me if it's gone?" And with a smile, he replied, "According to these numbers... YES!"

Tears of joy and relief overwhelmed me, and I found myself sobbing uncontrollably. Shaking and crying, I walked towards the nurse, and she gave me a tight hug. We went through a few more details, and then she asked me if I was ready to ring the bell. Without hesitation, I joyfully rang the bell, symbolizing the end of my battle and the beginning of a new chapter.

I embraced the moment for what it was, a celebration of my victory. The intensity of my emotions was just as strong as when I first received the diagnosis. Ironically, the fear remained the same, but I had done the work of renewing my mind, separating my story from my mom's. This allowed me to experience a sense of relief and gratitude.

Fast forward to March 2023, and I celebrated a year of being in remission. This journey has taught me that it's not just about surviving cancer; it's about thriving and reclaiming a healthy, wonderful life. I've learned that even in the moments when it feels like I'm alone, I am not. My relationship with God has grown stronger than ever before. He is my best friend; someone I can talk to about anything without fear of judgment. In His presence, I can be my authentic self. Recognizing His voice has been crucial in dispelling the feeling of loneliness. I now know that whenever I face fear, trouble, doubt, or discouragement, He is right there with me, residing within me.

Through this journey, I have discovered the strength of God within me by the way I have chosen to forgive others. It is a forgiveness that many may not understand, but it has brought me peace and freedom. I have also learned to love others, even those who may not deserve it in my eyes. This newfound understanding of myself and my relationship with God has empowered me to face challenges. I work diligently to release worries about things beyond my control and to embrace gratitude and gratefulness in every waking moment.

In the end, my victory over cancer has taught me the importance of cherishing life and finding joy in the present. I am determined to thrive, to live a healthy and wonderful life, and to be grateful for each day I am given.

I am filled with excitement as I embark on this new chapter of my life. I have grown stronger and more prepared for whatever lies ahead. While I may not know exactly what the future holds, I am confident in my obedience to follow the path that God has laid before me, and I trust that it will be amazing.

I am currently working as a life, relationship, and intimacy coach under my practice, Lending A Shoulder. My role involves assisting individuals in their pursuit of becoming the best versions of themselves. I find this work to be extremely fulfilling, as it allows me to make a positive impact on people's lives. In addition to my other projects, I run a podcast called The InSide Job Podcast Healed Inside Out. The podcast is a platform for people to share their journeys and testimonies and has proven to be incredibly liberating and helpful for many.

I place a high priority on taking care of my emotional, mental, and physical health, and I encourage others to do the same. Seeking help from therapists or doctors when needed is vital, and can be an important step toward a better, healthier life. It's important to ensure that everything is fine and to take the necessary steps towards achieving wellness.

I want to emphasize that I know I am not alone in my experiences of being molested, beaten, raped, hurt, rejected, suffering from depression, self-inflicted wounds, and afflictions. However, I have overcome these challenges and emerged as a stronger, wiser, and better woman today.

If you are going through a tough time, I want you to know that there is hope and help available to you. You can overcome all obstacles and heal. As I move forward, I remain open to the unknown future, knowing that my obedience to God's plan will lead me to greatness. I am grateful for the opportunity to serve as a coach and to provide a platform for others to share their stories and find healing. May blessings abound in all our journeys.

With love,
Nate'

www.ingramcontent.com/pod-product-compliance
Lightning Source LLC
Chambersburg PA
CBHW051816130726

47987CB00003B/1275